T0365443

The Little Lost Angel

Authored by Al Zepeda

Illustrated by Brendan Donegan

AuthorHouse™
1663 Liberty Drive
Bloomington, IN 47403
www.authorhouse.com
Phone: 1 (800) 839-8640

Scripture quotations marked NASB are taken from the New American Standard Bible®, Copyright © 1960, 1962, 1963, 1968, 1971, 1972, 1973, 1975, 1977, 1995 by The Lockman Foundation. Used by permission.

Published by AuthorHouse 03/05/2019

ISBN: 978-1-5462-7337-0 (sc)
ISBN: 978-1-5462-7339-4 (hc)
ISBN: 978-1-5462-7338-7 (e)

Library of Congress Control Number: 2018915007

Print information available on the last page.

Any people depicted in stock imagery provided by Getty Images are models, and such images are being used for illustrative purposes only. Certain stock imagery © Getty Images.

This book is printed on acid-free paper.

authorHOUSE®

The Little Lost Angel

Many years ago in a far away place, The Great and Mighty One created angels. There were many different sizes and types of angels designed for different things.

One of these angels was named Lucero. Although he was little for an angel, his joy would brighten up the stars and cause them to twinkle. Do you think you can find where he is in this galaxy on this page?

Lucero was created with a glow and he was warm, a joyful angel, that danced and jumped everywhere because he was full of happiness.

Lucero's task was, when The Great and Mighty One made a new star, Lucero would glow with tremendous heat to ensure the star would remain lit and stay bright.

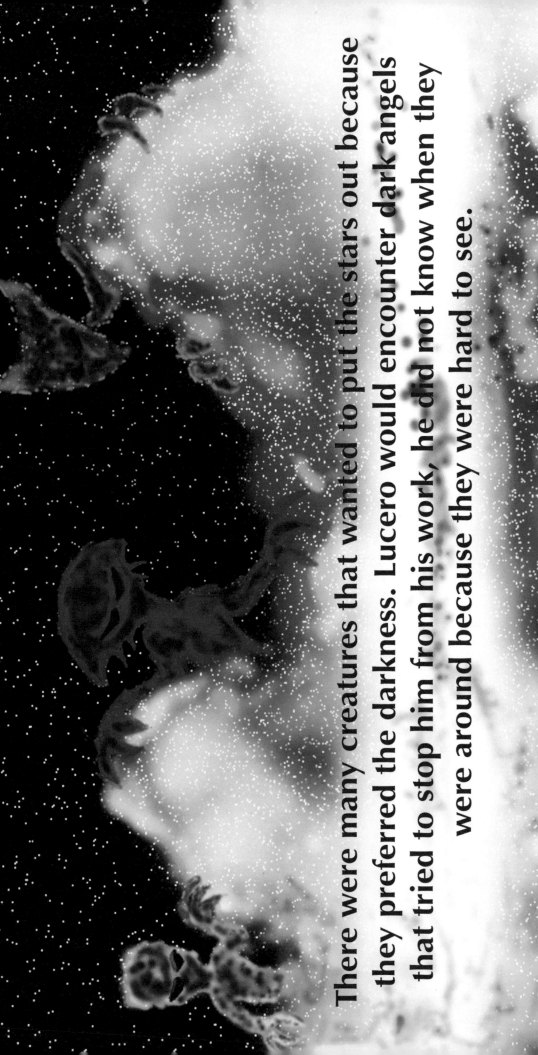

There were many creatures that wanted to put the stars out because they preferred the darkness. Lucero would encounter dark angels that tried to stop him from his work, he did not know when they were around because they were hard to see.

There were also little imps that tried to change his thoughts and distract him by asking him to play games so he would forget to do his work.

One day, Lucero was swinging from star to star, twirling with joy and dancing with glee.

...when a space storm blew him into a black hole!

In the black hole, Lucero could not tell up from down or one direction from another. He was lost for a very long time.

But Lucero never gave up hope. He continued to sing praises and worship the Great and Mighty One, God, and to be happy in whatever came his way.

One day he spotted a beam of light far away.

He decided to follow the light and knew in his heart that the light would take him home.

He was finally able to grab onto the beam of light as he flew out of the black hole. He rode this beam for a long time and remembered he had seen it before.

He finally landed with a **THUD!**

He peeked over the edge and saw a baby with people and animals gathered around.

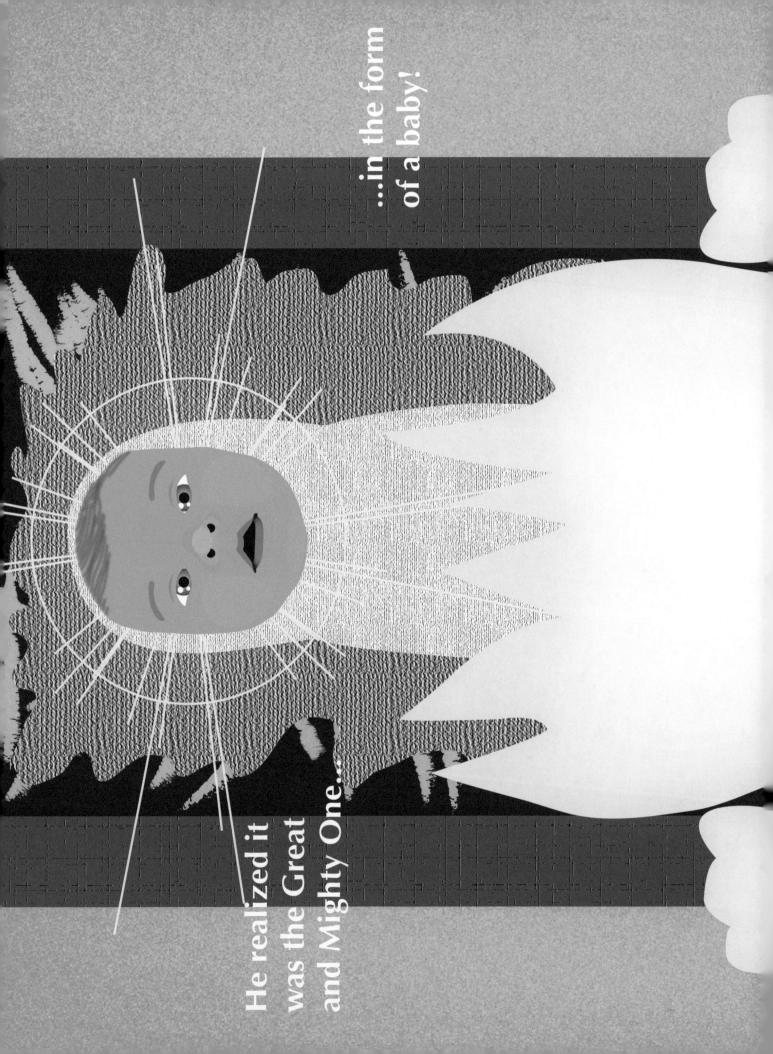

Lucero was so excited that he glowed more and more.
He provided warmth for the people and the animals.

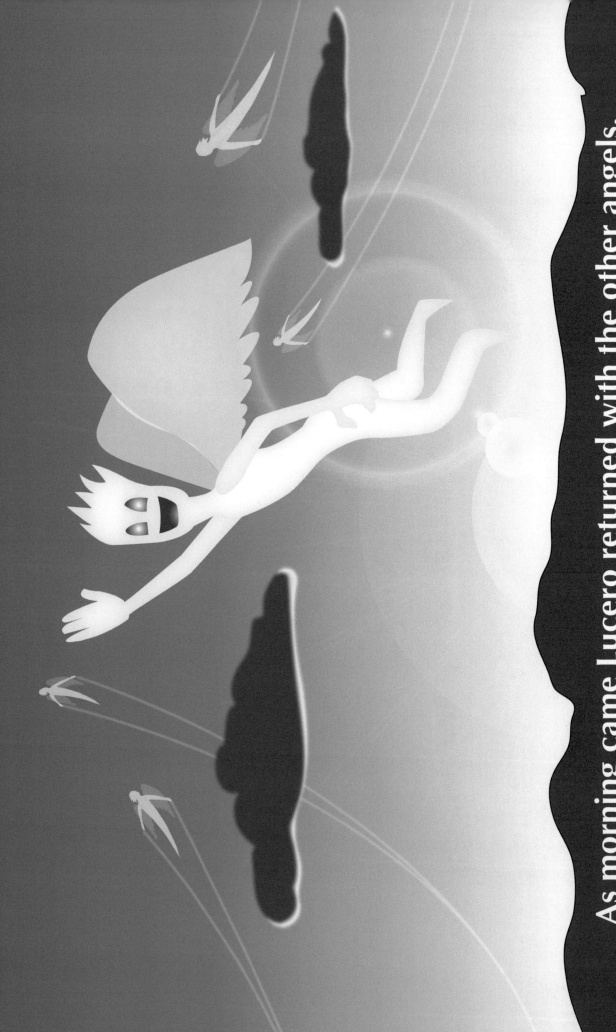

As morning came Lucero returned with the other angels.

Today, when you look up into the night sky, and see a star twinkling, you know it is Lucero, the little angel, doing his work for The Great and Mighty One.

The End.

Remember, no matter how dark and lonely things may be, God knows where you are and will help you out.

Joshua 1:9 " ...Be strong and courageous! Do not tremble or be dismayed, for the LORD your God is with you wherever you go." NASB

Printed in the United States
By Bookmasters